I0464192

The Authority Maker

How To Be The One Everyone Wants To Do Business With

by David DeSchoolmeester

Author, Speaker, Consultant

Copyright © 2014-2018 All rights reserved;
Your Authority Maker and David DeSchoolmeester

I dedicate this book to my wife, Wendy.

To the woman who makes me want
to be a better man.

A wife that stands by me and makes
life worth living every day!

TABLE OF CONTENTS

ABOUT THE AUTHOR

I'm not really comfortable talking about myself, but this is where it is expected, so here we go…

Hi, I am David DeSchoolmeester, a disabled veteran of the United States Navy who served my country for just over 12 years before being disabled and honorably discharged.

Originally I was trained in Nuclear Power Plant Operations by the Navy, but a disability took me away from that career. I attempted the same position in the Commercial Industry after the Navy, but my disability put me out of that career once again. It really sucks not being able to do what you enjoy doing for a living. Especially when it pays so well!

When I lost that position for a second time at the commercial nuclear power plant, I ended up in a clerical/administrative role supporting nuclear operations from a desk at a 40% pay cut! After a few years of little job growth or potential to grow, I decided to go back to Federal Government service where my previous military and some US Postal Service time gave me a total of some 17 years' Federal service on my first day back.

I began at the Department of Veterans Affairs, regained some of the money I had lost due to my disability in the nuclear industry. After several years though, I became very ill. I did not lose my job, but had to take a drastic pay decrease where I lost $33,000 per year in annual income and fell into a clerical position that I hated.

This illness took three years to get completely under control and regain my capacity for handling more developed work. During that three-year period, I lost the respect of my peers, as they watched my career crumble underneath me; I lost my marriage, as my wife decided "…in sickness and in health…" wasn't an oath she was willing to live up to; and of course the money I mentioned already.

Even after I regained the ability to perform work at a greater level than I was now at; the problem, I was still stuck in that position. I applied for numerous jobs, but local personnel did not want to take a chance on me due to my recent illness. Of course, none of them came right out and said this was the case, but after a while you just know what kind of mess you have found yourself in.

I knew that continuing to work for someone else, was not going to give me and my family what we deserve. I began to study as much as I could about Business, Marketing, Internet Marketing and Consulting. I earned a degree in Business Administration and one in Marketing, as well as a certificate in Business Analysis from George Washington University.

Having been in several industries in my life, with a great deal of experience and education, I felt that I could do well as a Business Consultant. I am also a published author and a lecturer.

I can be found at: http://www.yourauthoritymaker.com

I have a great deal to share in this eBook that I know you will want to take notes. I will also enjoy not saying the word "I" so much as we now jump into the world of "WE" and "YOU"

On a personal note, prayers are answered if you have a little faith. God found a wonderful woman for me – to whom I have dedicated this book. She's smart, funny, driven, and beautiful. We found each other on

Christian Mingle and have been happily married now for almost two years. I am so blessed to have her in my life!

INTRODUCTION

Ok, first of all, is it hard to build Authority and Credibility? No, given that you are a good person with no "skeletons" in the closet.

I have done this myself. I was diagnosed with Sleep Apnea in 1997. For many years it was kept in check with a Continuous Positive Air Pressure (CPAP) breathing device that I wear all night while I sleep. This book is not about Sleep Apnea, so I won't be going into great detail.

Several years ago, my Sleep Apnea got completely out of control and practically devastated my life. I discussed this in the previous chapter. It took three years to get it under control again, for which I am eternally grateful to my physician.

The point of this story is that a friend suggested I write about this three-year ordeal as a form of therapy. Well, I did and I felt that others needed to know about this and so I published that book (Sleep Apnea Dream Killer) on Amazon Kindle. I didn't advertise it, but others began to find it and through it they found me.

I began receiving periodic emails from people who have read it, mostly wanting more information. Since I am so passionate about this subject, I began to learn more and even interviewed my physician. I then wrote another book and joined various Facebook groups to help others and answer their questions.

I didn't set out to build Authority or Celebrity by writing the first book. As I said, it was for therapy and it helped me get over the events of those terrible three years.

However, one unexpected event happened and that was for people to be contacting me and asking me questions as though I was an expert. I am always careful to remind people that I am not a physician and they should always go to one to be evaluated.

This is when I learned about the power of writing and publishing a book to build Authority in a subject.

This book will not just discuss writing a book, as there are numerous ways to build Authority. Videos and Podcasts are also excellent ways and we will discuss all of them here for you.

You will learn about a five step method to build incredible Authority and Celebrity as well as how easy it really is to accomplish. Despite how easy it is, there are still very few people using these proven techniques.

The real question is, what about you?

I know you will enjoy this book, it's not very long because I hate all the added "fluff" that many writers bore their audience with. This is not a novel, so I will not write like it is. I have plenty of great information, without the creamy filler in between; thus allowing you to focus clearly on what is important.

After reading this book, you will have an actionable plan to move forward and grow your business exponentially.

REPUTATION MANAGEMENT IN THE DIGITAL AGE

Reputation Management is not just for business owners; it's really for anyone who is in the "Public Eye". For instance, politicians, local celebrities, government officials and of course our focus group of business owners.

A lot of people discount the importance of this one thing, until it becomes a problem. Don't wait until someone ruins your reputation that you will spend a lot of time attempting to fix. Take care of it now and monitor it.

Today, there are companies out there that do nothing but Reputation Management, because in the digital age, this is more important than you may think.

This section is about how to maintain a good image face-to-face and online (where it can really hurt you if you're not careful). A good reputation takes time to build and earn. However, a BAD reputation can be slapped on you overnight, while you sleep, and that's a big problem!

Prior to the "Information Age" one dissatisfied customer may tell a few friends and have minimal to moderate impact on your business and reputation. Conversely, with the advent of the Internet and the powerful effect of its Social Atmosphere, one dissatisfied customer can really cause a great deal of harm to your business and your personal reputation.

Today many people average 200 or more "Friends" or "Followers" on various social media like Facebook, Google+, Twitter and others. Some people have 500 to a thousand OR MORE!

One Tweet and subsequent Re-Tweets can be a powerful weapon against your bottom line, unless you take precautions upfront to aid in Damage Control! I can't say this strong enough – Get Serious About Reputation Management!

Going forward, we're going to discuss ways in which:

- You can see what your current reputation is,
- You can set up an automatic monitor for your reputation,
- You can create a positive reputation, and
- You can repair your reputation if the worst happens and you fall under attack.

Here are some ways in which you can see what the current "buzz" is about you and your business:

- Perform an exact phrase search for your name and then for your business name in the search engines. You do this by putting quotes in front and behind your name and then clicking the search button. For instance my name is David DeSchoolmeester, so on Google, I would type in "David DeSchoolmeester" and click the Search button. This will bring back a listing of every web page, document and post with your search term exactly. So, any web page with the exact phrase of David DeSchoolmeester will be listed. Do this for both your full name and then your business name. See my example below.

- Check sites like Yelp.com; AngiesList.com; Google Local Reviews; Yahoo Local; and Bing Local for anything they might have from customers or people who have met you. These are common review sites.

- Check Industry Specific review sites, for example a doctor or dentist may want to check a site called HealthGrades.com for reviews. I have a dentist client who had no idea he had eight 5-star reviews from patients on HealthGrades.com until I checked this for him. Once I showed him these reviews, we put a link to them on his webpage so that he could use the power of Positive Social Proof to his favor. Just that one thing put him up on the number one spot of Google search engine results page.

So, now that I have checked the current situation, how do I monitor it as time goes forward?

Great question, I'm really glad you asked.

Google has actually given us a FREE Tool that we can use every day to automatically search the Internet for us. It's called Google Alerts and is found at http://www.google.com/alerts/

Go to the Google Alerts page, then set up a search for your full name and a separate one for your business name. You can have Google email you as soon as something is uploaded, or on any other frequency of your choosing.

You can set up as many of these Alerts as you like, and even check on your competition in business or for specific product terms so that you can stay on top of the latest innovations. The first time you use this, you will see the most current results, which will aid you in determining a base for how you are perceived.

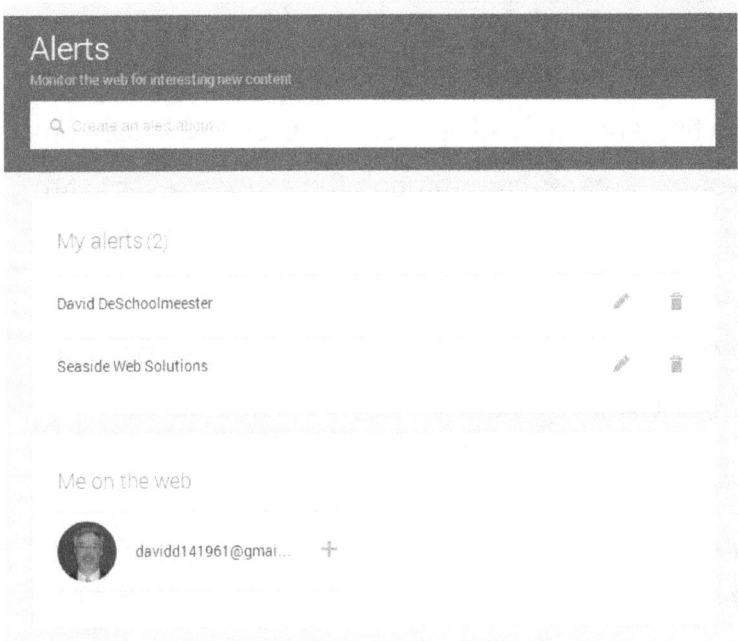

Okay, now what can I do to create a positive reputation or image?

The number one thing everybody should do is to have a great quality product or service with great customer service. Quality and consistency. Quality will bring people in, consistency with great customer service will keep them coming back.

For instance, I went to 5-minute Oil Change the other day. The service was top-notch, they took good care of me and my car. They know that service starts and ends with "ME", the customer.

I was offered a complimentary beverage while I was waiting and the lead technician {excuse the play on words} "steered" me through the process every step of the way. When he discussed one oil over another and updated me on my air filter, fluid levels, and tire pressures, I had no problem paying a little more for the better oil whether it was really better or not.

That was because the customer service was outstanding. The best part is, every time I go there, the service is always outstanding. That's what keeps me coming back, over and over again. When you experience this time and time again, you feel relaxed, comfortable and grow trust that builds bonds.

Another thing you can do is to create an account on review sites like Yelp.com with information about your business, location and website. Give people a place to leave reviews, especially the happy customers. Then, provide a link on your website and your physical locations, to this and other review sites you have an account with.

One thing I saw someone do, that makes great sense, is to have a sign at your physical business location [and/or your website if you are totally online] that reads: "If we haven't earned a 5-Star rating on Yelp.com from you today, let us know what we can do to make things right, before you leave."

Just having a statement like this staring your customers/clients/patients in the face will do two things:

1. It will let your customer know you really care and hopefully open their mouths to you before they go out and recklessly cause harm to your reputation. Their dissatisfaction may have been a complete misunderstanding and you can fix it, On The Spot!

2. It will let your customer know they can go on Yelp.com and give you a good review in writing on the Internet. This is something you can link to and use in your advertising.

You can also create a Facebook, Twitter and LinkedIn account for your business, but don't do this unless you plan to be active on them. An inactive social media page for your business does not invoke a very positive image for you.

Remember, these sites are for being social, especially Facebook, sharing information and having FUN. They are NOT for selling anything and you can upset people very quickly when you violate this unwritten rule.

Now, how do I fix a problem with my reputation from bad reviews?

First off, you need to reach out to that person as soon as possible! People need to see that you are at least attempting to resolve a problem that has become public. Every attempt to resolve the problem is vitally important because the problem is "public" and complete strangers will judge you on how you handle (or how they see you handle) the situation.

A little extra time and effort on your part goes a long way, as others will see this as well.

For the most part, people are generally good and taking the time to reach out to them, trying to resolve the situation, give them a refund or replace the product will make things right.

If you have satisfied the customer, ask them nicely to either remove the bad review, or if it cannot be removed, ask them to now place a positive review to refute the one they first left.

I think you will find that when they see you going the extra mile to satisfy them, that will often times be enough for them to change their mind and see that they may have been too hasty in their criticism.

However, if you have done everything humanly possible, and the situation has not changed; apologize, tell them you are sorry they feel that way, and leave it alone ('cuz that's the truth – you sure didn't set out to cause anyone to dislike your business).

It's very important that they know you tried, even though they still hold you in contempt. AND most importantly the others who see the original bad review will also see your attempts and, in turn, you diffuse the bad review.

If and when the day arrives that someone posts a negative review about your business and a satisfied customer comes to your rescue…you've arrived!

This is the ultimate in damage control!

It's one thing for you to attempt to appease the dissatisfied customer, but to have one, two, or more of your super satisfied customers come to your rescue, speaks volumes.

Damage Control does not get any better than that!

Of course you don't just leave it to that, if it happens. You need to reach out, publicly, to this person and ask, privately, what actually happened. Get all the facts and then offer to resolve it.

Remember a Good Reputation takes time to build, but a bad one only takes seconds to cause incredible damage to your business.

You now know how to Manage Your Business and Personal Reputation.

THE VALUE EQUATION

This concept comes from one of the most well-known and respected Internet Marketers – Frank Kern.

Because he understands this equation and the power of Authority, he is one of the highest priced business consultants and has people waiting in line to hire him.

$$\text{Practical Value} + \text{Intrinsic Value} = \text{TOTAL PERCEIVED VALUE}$$

Practical Value is the product or service you provide. Chances are this does not differ much from those that your peers provide. So these differences are normally minimal.

Intrinsic Value is the unseen value that is created by Positioning and Promotion. This is where the big differences are between someone who charges $50 for their service and someone who charges $250 for the same service and has more satisfied customers/clients/patients.

Here's an example:

A Rolls Royce Ghost sells for $300,000

while a BMW 750 sells for only $100,000.

Why? The practical value differences are minimal:
BMW owns Rolls Royce, the Ghost chassis is
practically the same as the BMW 750. But Rolls
Royce can charge 300% more.

The difference is in the Intrinsic Value of the Rolls
Royce brand. It is Positioned as the BEST.

As an owner, you are treated differently if you pull up
to a meeting in a Rolls than in a BMW. You are
viewed differently, people notice this car, and see you
as a SUCCESS just for driving one.

This Positioning is costing an additional $200,000 to
the Rolls Royce Ghost owner.

Building Authority positively affects your Positioning
which increases your Intrinsic Value – ultimately

increasing your Total Perceived Value in the marketplace. Increase your Intrinsic Value and you Increase Your Demand!

How about another example:

New Ferrari's sell out immediately at $50,000 to $65,000 above sticker price because of the Intrinsic Value of owning one;

People stand in long lines for new iPhones ----> Positioning ---> increased Intrinsic Value.

Do you want to whip your marketplace up into a frenzy?

Do you want to make your fans love you that much?

The fastest way for people like you and me, those who do NOT have hundreds of thousands or millions of dollars for massive ad campaigns, is to build your Authority in your market. This is not difficult and is relatively easy and in-expensive.

Multicasting is how it is done and I describe it in detail in the very next chapter...

MULTICAST MARKETING

> This methodology helps you soar
> above all the rest of your peers
> within your industry/field of work.
>
> You're about to discover a system
> that will put you on level playing
> ground with the best of the best in
> your field and soar above all of
> your peers.

You Everywhere NOW is the concept that makes this all happen for you. Just like it says – Multicasting is about getting your message everywhere on the Internet so that it can be read, seen and heard; anywhere, on any device, anytime. This theory is also the ultimate in Search Engine Optimization, or SEO because of its ability to get your message out to many outlets on the Internet and in many different formats.

Recent changes in Google's analytical software have proven that Search Engine Optimizers (people who perform SEO) who rely on tips and tricks; will not last long.

Although, they are not hurting themselves as much as they are hurting their customers.

When a search engine (maybe Google) finds disreputable actions by an SEO, it becomes the business owner's problem, and does not affect the so-called "expert SEO". What I mean by that is the business owner paying for the services takes the hit on his website and the SEO just moves on to another client. But the "hit" could be anything from losing a couple of spots of positioning in search engine results or as bad as being DE-LISTED!

I explained this in better detail in my previous book "Internet Marketing and Search Engine Optimization – A Brief Guide for High-end Professionals". Check out the link, in the back of this book, to where you can get a copy for yourself.

You Everywhere NOW helps you to have a widespread Internet presence that Google finds, likes, and rewards. The "guts" of the system and how You Everywhere Now works is called "Multicasting".

Multicasting helps to expand your Internet presence, not only all over the Internet, but it also makes your content available in multiple formats. By "changing up" and existing throughout the Internet on numerous and varied formats, you gain favor in Google's analytical software – therefore getting you better rankings in organic search results.

Multicasting allows you to create content once, and distribute everywhere to every device, anywhere at any time.

First let's look at some data:

- 61% of American adults own a Smartphone, and that number is growing
- 93% of smartphone owners say they use their devices for "accessing content and information"
- There are 70 Million active Pinterest users
- 5,700 Tweets happen every second
- Users share 2.5 Billion pieces of content each day on Facebook
- Google+ is growing rapidly with 925,000 new users every day

- 75% of LinkedIn users are 35 years old or older
- Amazon's current annual revenue from book sales is $5.25 Billion
- 30.6% of Americans own an eReading device
- Amazon has close to 300 Million credit cards on file

Why Do People Use The Internet? To get FREE information, right?

This gives Professionals, like you, an excellent opportunity by providing the information they are looking for, at no cost. You are the "Expert" in your field and when you give people what they want for free, they will reward you when it comes time to utilize that information, by choosing you; the person who provided the information up front. That is called "Reciprocity".

By giving them the "what", not necessarily the "how to", you are building a "trust bond" with them. When they need services that you perform, they will remember and reward that trust bond, by coming to you for that service.

Before I go any further, let me first explain testing results from Dr. Albert Mehrabian.

Dr. Mehrabian performed studies to determine the percentages of effective types of communication.

He found that:

- 7% of communication are the actual "words" that are used;
- 38% of communication are the "vocal elements" (such as tone of voice, voice inflection, etc);
- 55% of communication are "non-verbal" (such as how you move your hands, the look on your face, your general posture, and much more)

So we find that if we use just a newsletter (or book, like this one) we are achieving only 7% of the potential for effective communication; if we use audio we are achieving 38%; but if we use VIDEO, we achieve 93% of the potential for effective communication.

Multicasting actually allows you to obtain 100%! So, let's get back to it...

How do you build the trust bond we mentioned earlier? By Multicasting, it should be noted that it is not necessary to do all 5 of the following steps to find success:

WARNING! DO NOT be scared off by thinking this is too difficult, uncomfortable, or time consuming.

90% of Multicasting can be outsourced while still giving you 100% control over the entire process.

#1 Livecasting

The first step should be Livecasting. In other words, it is creating a "Live" broadcast (hence the term Livecasting), over the Internet for your target audience. That broadcast is recorded and later gets uploaded as a video, so everyone can access it on any device, at anytime, anywhere. It leverages an existing infrastructure to expand your business reach to all of YouTube's, Vimeo's, and Daily Motion's members.

Live is a powerful format, as you can interact with your audience. Don't worry, if you're uncomfortable in front of a camera, this can be outsourced.

Live, forces attention from your consumer to you. Because it's live, this format creates excitement in your audience and it pushes you to create content, moving your business forward.

Live also creates a buzz – When you know an audience is watching you live and that you're interacting with them directly, it becomes infectious.

Livecasting then creates the material for the other steps in the Multicasting system. This is the only content you will have to create from scratch.

#2 Podcasting

The second step in Multicasing is the Podcast. A Podcast is a downloadable radio or television (video) show, episode or series that has 100% deliverability and automated subscription options.

This is NOT live. We simply take the audio out of the Livecasting video created in the previous step and upload it to make it available to over 1 Billion iPad, iPod, Apple TV and iPhone users.

Automation is the key. Once someone subscribes to your Podcast channel they get a notice every time a new Podcast episode has been uploaded. Also,

Apple does not limit the number of shows you can create so, you could start a radio or TV network for FREE.

AND, you can monetize your podcasts with sponsors, advertising revenue, or income from leads and direct sales.

#3 Socialcasting

This is the act of building your audience by distributing your content across different social media networks.

Once again, we Socialcast the same video created in the Livecast, so no new development needs to be done. We also Socialcast the Podcast episodes once they are uploaded to let others (who are not subscribed to our Podcast yet) know about the latest installment. You never know what topic will really pull in a new Podcast subscriber.

By utilizing the power of social media, Socialcasting allows you to partner with multibillion-dollar organizations and brands in order to deliver your message to their audiences. Brands like Facebook, Twitter, Pinterest, Delicious, Vimeo, YouTube, and many more.

Meet your clients or patients where they already are – on their favorite social network.

#4 Bookcasting

This takes the same content from the Livecast, or new content in the same category. You convert it into a book or white paper to be sold or given away in both digital and physical form.

Bookcasting provides another format to reach your target audience. It leverages a multibillion-dollar network – Amazon - that has close to 300 million credit cards on file and allows you to make a profit on your original content.

Publishing a book creates instant credibility and authority, giving your audience the perception of your increased expertise.

Everyone wants to do business with the person who "Wrote The Book" on the subject they are most interested in.

Amazon will give you a traffic producing, optimized website free and pay you 70% commissions each time they sell your book. It's so easy a 9-year old girl (Abbey Richter) wrote 4 books in 4 months and is being featured on a cover of a magazine and being asked to speak and do book signings with her mom.

Books are THE IDEAL way to build AUTHORITY for you, your brand, and your business.

WARNING! REMEMBER, DO NOT be scared off by thinking this is too difficult, uncomfortable, or time consuming.

90% of Multicasting can be outsourced while still giving you 100% control over the entire process.

Once the initial Livecast is complete, most of the rest of the system uses that same content!

#5 Mobilecasting

This is where even more MONEY is made. 73% of the human race uses social media, but almost 80% have a mobile phone. More than half of all social media users use their phones or tablets to connect. However, less than 22% of all websites are really "Mobile Ready".

Does your website reformat automatically to adjust to the size of the browser window on whatever device people are viewing it from? If not, you could be missing out on a lot of potential visitors.

Google receives over 5 Billion searches every day; 55% of those searches are local searches; 43% of those local searches are performed on mobile devices (that equates to 1.2 Billion local searches each day from mobile devices) and that number increases every day.

Make sure your website and content can be seen appropriately on the one device 61% of American adults have in their pocket...their Smart Phone.

Most businesses are only capturing leads with one "channel" – email on a lead capture form – and most of these pages are NOT mobile responsive and don't work well on a tablet or phone.

These businesses are leaving 60% of additional money on the "sales table".

You can use your Livecasts, Podcasts, Bookcasts and Socialcasts to capture leads and make sales. Just one of these methods can make a big difference in your business and your life. Remember what I told you about people reaching out to me just from the Sleep Apnea book I wrote?

That was just for therapy. What if I "monetized" that for profit as well?

Using Multicasting helps you Capture Leads via:

- Mobile responsive web pages
    - Desktop and laptop computers
    - Smartphones
    - Tablets
- Mobile text messages
- Short codes
- Automated voice calls
- QR Codes
- Business card scans

Then you can Connect or Follow up with:

- Email
- A mobile text message
- Voicemail
- Video
- Audio message
- Podcast directly to their computer, tablet, smartphone, car or TV in their living room

This is a real Game Changer and the Future of Marketing and SEO. Don't put yourself at the mercy of an "expert SEO" who most likely is violating the terms of Google and other top search engines.

Multicasting can really make all the difference in the world to getting you noticed as an AUTHORITY.

WHAT SHOULD I WRITE ABOUT

The first recommendation I have is to do what is called the 10 x 10. You take the top 10 Frequently Asked Questions (FAQ) and 10 "Should Asked Questions" (SAQ) and put together a series of 20 short videos.

The FAQ's are the most frequent questions you hear from your prospects/clients/patients. We are all used to seeing these on many websites we visit. It's important that you use video, to really connect with your audience. Remember, do you want to be 93% effective at communicating or just 7%, like most other people using text only to respond to FAQ's?

The SAQ's allow you to really point out what is unique about YOU, why people should do business with YOUR, services/products YOU offer that no one else does, etc. It gives YOU the ability to ask and answer questions that YOU wish your clients/patients asked, but didn't. YOU have "carte blanche" to mold a potential client/patient into how you want them to think of YOU and YOUR brand. These are the most important videos out of the 20.

You do not have to do these as a Livecast, but merely provide a place to where viewers can watch them from your website. Of course, we would also Socialcast them to the many video and non-video social sites to give you the greatest reach.

Other topics you may want to write about are specific White Papers that you have authored or co-authored, especially if it is about a new service/product/treatment that you helped to perfect. You will want to write about unique certifications you have or achievements you have accomplished. We would then get these listed in a Press Release for your business.

You would want to write about specific successes you have had, describing in detail what it was and why it is so important. You may also want to do a monthly Podcast or Bookcast where your customers/clients/patients have input to lead you to understand what they are interested in and then you answer it.

Each one of these could be turned into a document that can be released through Amazon, Google Play or via your own site. Each time a release of new information is made a Socialcast is performed to get the word out and increase your reach throughout the Internet. These releases and Socialcasts will each have a positive effect on your website's ranking in the search engines.

It would be a good idea to create videos from each of these and Socialcast them as well.

Books are not as difficult to create or publish as we once thought. They also don't have to be massive documents hundreds of pages long either. As a matter of fact, a long book like that is the last thing you want to publish to aid in building your Authority. No one will want to read a novel-sized ebook like that.

Remember who you are writing for, your customers/clients/patients. You are not writing to impress your peers; at least that is NOT the kind of writing we are talking about in this book.

You are writing to bring value and goodwill to your customers/clients/patients and to grow that audience as large as you can. So, you do not want to talk over their heads with a bunch of highly technical terms, legal or medical "mumbo-jumbo". It's ok to have a little bit of that in what you write, always making sure to define those terms. However, too much of that and your target audience will get bored or worse yet, think that you are just trying to show off. If that happens they will leave you flat.

You are in business, or have your own practice, to serve others. So, that is who you must always be thinking about, especially in every word you write, video and/or Podcast you create.

If you always stay focused on your audience, you will do just fine. Give them what they want and you will be rewarded.

WHAT KIND OF VIDEO SHOULD I USE

There are several different styles of shooting a video. I'm just going to discuss a small handful here, as these are the most typical and work the best for Livecasting.

The Livecast video (10 x 10) will be approximately 1-hour long, as it will be answering 20 different FAQ's and SAQ's. From this, it will be broken down into smaller chunks for the Podcasts. 1 question per Podcast episode.

If you are selling or teaching a long topic, it would be good to cut it into chunks that are easily understandable. Besides 10 videos each 18 to 20 minutes long seems like a better value than 1 long 200-minute video teaching the same thing. It's that perceived value that you want along with real value to keep your audience happy.

In any video you have eight (8) seconds to capture their attention. So, don't waste four or five seconds on fancy graphic depicting your logo or video title. If you really want to show this, intro the video first to capture the attention of your audience, segue into the graphic and then back into the video.

That first eight seconds is too important to waste.

The Interview

The first video method I am going to discuss is the Interview. Preferably you would be interviewed by a person known and respected by your target audience. This way you can "borrow" their Authority or Celebrity at the same time building your own. However, if that is not possible, an unknown person would do just as well.

After all, you are the important person in this interview. When doing an interview, you will need more than one camera angle. You will need one on the interviewer and one on the interviewee.

Promoting a new book or some other special event may be a good reason to use the Interview format, but it is not a good method for teaching something like you would in your FAQ / SAQ videos.

The Talking Head

This format is mostly of one, sometimes two, subjects talking directly into the camera. Periodically it is acceptable to change the view to the computer screen or other source, especially when showing an example via your laptop screen.

This is an acceptable format for teaching a subject as in your FAQ / SAQ videos. It is especially helpful when you want your audience to connect with you, a very powerful effect.

It requires only one camera and mostly just one subject talking. It cannot be understated at the power of connecting and bonding with your audience. Your entire focus is on answering the questions they need to hear about. They will look upon you as an authority figure who is giving them the value they are looking for at no cost. This builds that "Trust Bond". By using subtitles or overlays in the video to highlight the most important parts you can move from 93% effective communication to 100%!

The Read & Speak

For the most part, this format does not require a camera at all. This requires screen capture software and a microphone. The audience sees a presentation that is narrated by you, but typically they do not see you.

I do NOT recommend this for your videos, especially ones where you are attempting to connect and build Authority with your target audience. This is still very popular with Internet Marketers where many times a personal connection is already made or not as important as the "hype" they may be attempting to achieve.

My personal preference for building Authority and the FAQ / SAQ videos is the "Talking Head" format. It is more than acceptable to combine this with the "Read & Speak" for those times when you need to show a graphic, like a chart or table to get your point across.

For building Authority and establishing a connection to your audience, there is nothing better than the "Talking Head" format.

There are many other types and styles of videos that we did not discuss here. A quick Google search will provide a great deal of information, but the styles discussed here are more than sufficient to serve the purposes we have.

CASE STUDY:

Here is a Case Study about a two location Veterinary Hospital that receives an average of 1,000 phone calls per month for information and new patient requirements. The income of this hospital is approximately $480,000 per year. Each new client/customer adds $200 to the office on the first appointment (on average).

The receptionists each close an average of 20% of the calls for new patient care, where the Veterinarian consistently closes 90%.

Sticking to our Multicasting model, the hospital currently has a list of 15 to 20 Frequently Asked Questions & Should Ask Questions (FAQ/SAQ).

LIVECASTING:

We would hold a 1-hour LIVECAST Question & Answer session covering these 15 to 20 FAQ/SAQ

The Veterinarian does the LIVECAST personally, because he is the one who closes 90% of the calls and people want to hear from the expert.

Each question will take approximately two to three minutes each, for a total of 60 to 90 minutes.

This Livecast will be scheduled one week to one month out, providing time to SOCIALCAST the link to live event and build an audience. A poster should be put up at the physical locations.

Once the Livecast is complete, it can be downloaded to a VIDEO.

PODCASTING:

Then we strip out the audio from this video and make 15 to 20 PODCAST Episodes. Add the following to each Podcast:

- A short "Bumper" on front end of each podcast – logo and possibly a brief animation.
- A Banner on the lower 3rd of video; which will include the name of the Veterinarian: Dr. Vet name and name of business
- Free music to each podcast from YouTube or another source for the background

SOCIALCAST:

Besides the Socialcasting done to promote the Livecast, we would Socialcast to promote each Podcast episode – dispense every two to three days to last about a month.

And Socialcast to promote the Bookcast below.

BOOKCAST:

Transcribe the Livecast video into a book format, adding a "Forward", "Introduction", and information about the business, then publish 1 book every 2 months.

One Livecast each month can produce:

- 12 Livecasts in a year
- 180 to 240 Podcast episodes in a year
- 6 Books in a year

Simply repeat the LIVECAST / PODCASTS / BOOKCAST sequence each month

Also, create a Membership site for access to all videos in one location. You can even charge a small fee for access and add new videos each month from each Livecast. Make it FREE for 7 days and then $7 per month afterwards.

This can easily turn a local physical business into an International Training Business – LIVECASTS, PODCASTS, BOOKS, and the Membership site.

Another way to promote new business is to have the receptionist get the address of each new person that calls in (not necessarily current customers) and send out the latest book for FREE. Have Dr. Vet sign each one, and the receptionist mails each one out for under $5 per book (including the price of the book).

This creates tremendous Goodwill and promotes the position of Authority onto the Veterinarian.

SUMMARY:

- Quadruple the conversion rates over what the receptionists were converting by putting Dr. Vet on the LIVECASTS and PODCASTS.
- Create MASSIVE content and Goodwill through LIVECASTS, PODCASTS, BOOKS, Membership Site.
- Create HUGE Authority for Dr. Vet. After all, who throws out a book that has been signed?

FINANCIAL RESULTS:

How many extra appointments would be created with this model?

Let's use a very conservative number of new clients to this system.

NOW

1,000 calls / month = 200 new clients / month = $200 / client = = $40,000 per month

Model adds

100 new clients / month = $200 / client = = $20,000 per month

That's a $240,000 per year increase!!!

10% of 1,000 joins membership ~ 1,200 in 1st year x $7 / month = = $8,400 / month (conservative)

ADDING $28,400 per month means an **additional**

$340,800 per year!

As your consultant, I will take care of:

- Promoting and helping to write each LIVECAST
- Breakdown the Livecasts and create each PODCAST
- Transcribe and write each BOOK
- Create the Membership Site
- SOCIALCASTING for promoting each step of the Multicasting Model.
- As well as develop other new projects to continue to add more and more business for you.

The business would:

- Business Owner performs one 1-hour Q&A session (Livecast) each month
- Receptionists send out books to new potential clients calling in

HOW DO I GET ALL THIS DONE?

WARNING – Shameless Plug Ahead…

That's the easy part. Your Authority Maker can take care of all your Multicasting needs.
As a matter of fact, why don't you get your first 1-on-1 Consultation FREE?

Find out what David and Your Authority Maker can do for you and your business – You'll Be Amazed!

Click Here Now:

http://www.yourauthoritymaker.com/application/

You'll get a FREE 1-on-1 Consultation with David, where he will give you an immediately actionable plan to help your business grow. NO STRINGS ATTACHED!

TO SUM IT ALL UP

Well, like I said, it is a short book; but we covered a lot of material. I know you will find this useful in your business going forward.

So what did we discuss?

- We talked about me (the part I hate, but it may be useful for some of you who may associate with one or more of my experiences)
- We talked about Reputation Management and how important it is in the Digital Age
- We talked about Multicasting. What it is, the five steps involved and how important it is to building relationships with your target audience
- We talked about what you should write about to build Authority with your customers/clients/patients
- Then we discussed a few styles of videos and what is best for our purpose
- We then talked about a Case Study showing how Multicasting added between **$340,800 per year** to a Veterinary Hospital
- Then I gave you a shameless plug for my services if you are ready to make this happen

for you. I also gave you some Freebies for you to get a little touch of some of the topics we talked about.

So, now it's time to make it happen. Having Authority in your chosen field could make the difference between prospective customers/clients/patients picking you or a competitor to do business with.

Use this information and I know it will drive more traffic to you and help you serve more people.

Take Care

God Bless You and Your Business,

David DeSchoolmeester

OTHER BOOKS BY DAVID DESCHOOLMEESTER

Below is a list of other Business and Non-Business books I have written. All are available on Amazon Kindle via the links provided…

Business:

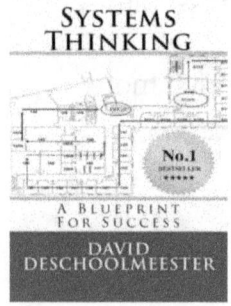

Systems Thinking A Blueprint For Success (https://www.createspace.com/5001918)

-   This book discusses the great need for systematizing your business NOW! Small Business owners have really taken a hit in the last decade and this book will take a look at why and what the small business owner should do about it. Follow the most successful business model in the world!

Reinvent Yourself And Survive Today's Economy

(http://www.amazon.com/dp/B007HB8HGY)

- Throughout my working life I have had to "Reinvent" myself many times, for one reason or another. In this book, I discuss those reinventions and how to go about doing it for yourself to give yourself a new fresh start. You may be forced into it, due to the economy and corporate downsizing, but there is a way to help yourself through it.

Internet Marketing And Search Engine Optimization – A Guide For High-end Professionals

(https://www.createspace.com/5019986)

- This book is a very short guide designed to education busy professionals, like Lawyers,

Physicians, Surgeons, Dentists, etc. You are way too busy to have to learn how to market and advertise your practice on your own, but today that is just what many of you need to do. This book will help to teach you some things you need to know in order to hire the right person to promote your practice like it should be promoted.

Non-Business

Sleep Apnea Dream Killer

(https://www.createspace.com/4996516)

- This is a detailed description of a 3-year period of my life when my Sleep Apnea became wildly out of control and the depression that caused me to nearly take my own life. I lost my position at work, $33,000 per year in income; lost the respect of my peers; lost the respect of my own daughter; lost my marriage.

Sleep Apnea Effects

(https://www.createspace.com/4989907)

- I performed a great deal of research for this book. It lists all kinds of affects that Sleep Apnea has on your body. Does Sleep Apnea kill? Not directly, but there are numerous ways in which it can indirectly – the kind of things you'd be a fool to disregard. Also inside this book are the transcripts of an Interview I had with the Head of Pulmonology at Tulane University School of Medicine and Sleep Lab.

www.ingramcontent.com/pod-product-compliance
Lightning Source LLC
Chambersburg PA
CBHW071726170526
45165CB00005B/2180